SPOTLIGHT ON THE RISE AND FALL OF ANCIENT CIVILIZATIONS

ANCIENT CHINESE DAILY LIFE

MARCIA AMIDON LUSTED

ROSEN PUBLISHING
New York

Published in 2017 by The Rosen Publishing Group, Inc.
29 East 21st Street, New York, NY 10010

Copyright © 2017 by The Rosen Publishing Group, Inc.

First Edition

All rights reserved. No part of this book may be reproduced in any form without permission in writing from the publisher, except by a reviewer.

Library of Congress Cataloging-in-Publication Data

Names: Lusted, Marcia Amidon, author.
Title: Ancient Chinese daily life / Marcia Amidon Lusted.
Description: First edition. | New York : Rosen Publishing, 2017. | Series: Spotlight on the rise and fall of ancient civilizations | Includes bibliographical references and index. | Audience: Grades 7-12.
Identifiers: LCCN 2016004997| ISBN 9781477788882 (library bound) | ISBN 9781477788868 (pbk.) | ISBN 9781477788875 (6-pack)
Subjects: LCSH: China--Social life and customs--To 221 B.C.
Classification: LCC DS741.65 .L87 2016 | DDC 931--dc23
LC record available at http://lccn.loc.gov/2016004997

Manufactured in the United States of America

CONTENTS

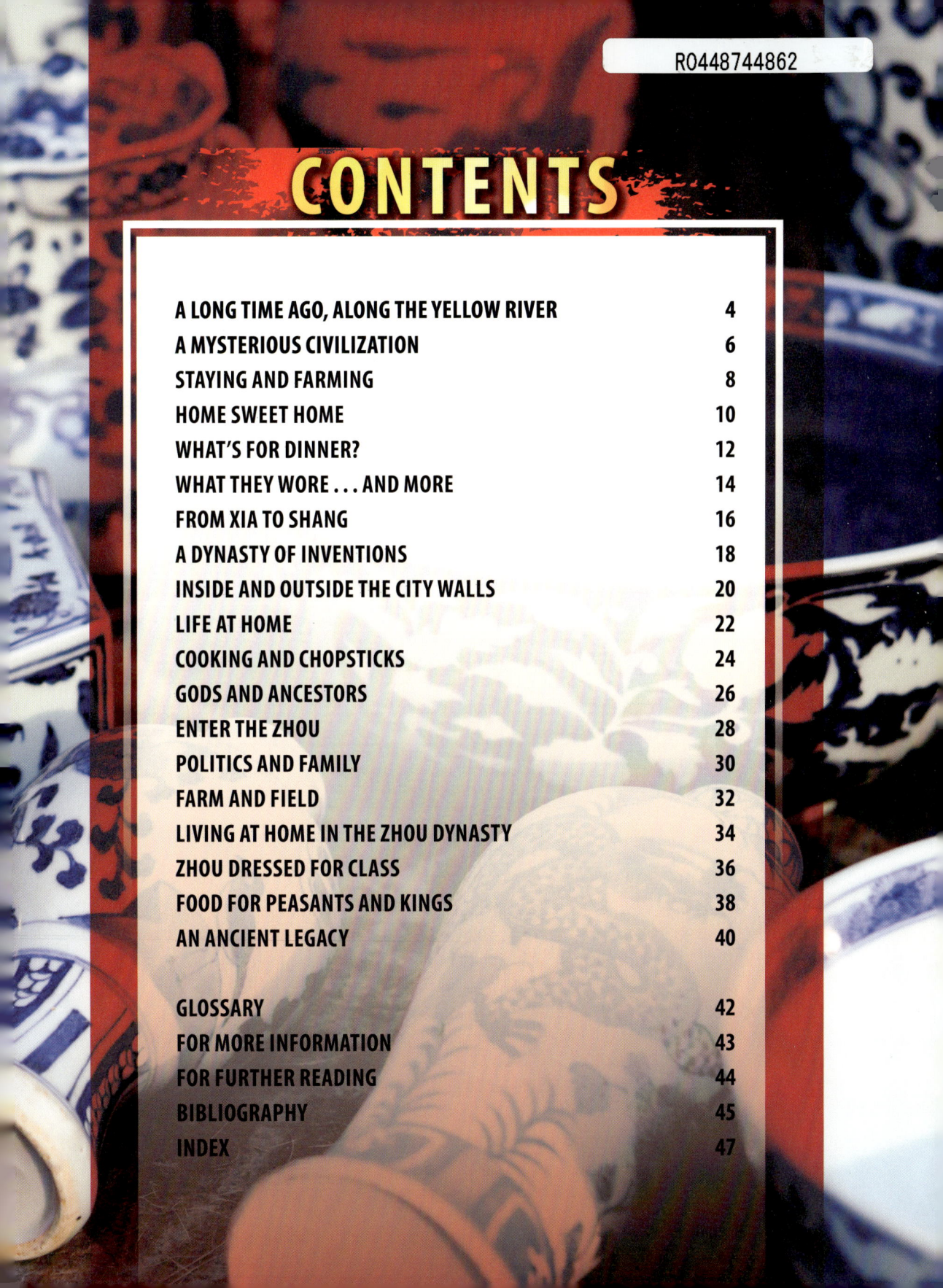

A LONG TIME AGO, ALONG THE YELLOW RIVER	4
A MYSTERIOUS CIVILIZATION	6
STAYING AND FARMING	8
HOME SWEET HOME	10
WHAT'S FOR DINNER?	12
WHAT THEY WORE . . . AND MORE	14
FROM XIA TO SHANG	16
A DYNASTY OF INVENTIONS	18
INSIDE AND OUTSIDE THE CITY WALLS	20
LIFE AT HOME	22
COOKING AND CHOPSTICKS	24
GODS AND ANCESTORS	26
ENTER THE ZHOU	28
POLITICS AND FAMILY	30
FARM AND FIELD	32
LIVING AT HOME IN THE ZHOU DYNASTY	34
ZHOU DRESSED FOR CLASS	36
FOOD FOR PEASANTS AND KINGS	38
AN ANCIENT LEGACY	40
GLOSSARY	42
FOR MORE INFORMATION	43
FOR FURTHER READING	44
BIBLIOGRAPHY	45
INDEX	47

A LONG TIME AGO, ALONG THE YELLOW RIVER

China is one of the four most ancient civilizations in the world. Its huge area is home to many different groups of people. It also has many different climates and terrains. Humans first appeared in China during the Paleolithic era, as long as 200,000 years ago. They were hunter-gatherers who preyed on animals for meat and also ate what plants they could find. By 10,000 BCE humans in China began to grow food, the beginnings of agriculture. By 5,000 BCE they were building settlements. Soon they would be taming animals like pigs and cattle.

In most ancient cultures, civilization began in the valleys that surrounded major rivers. In China, it began along the Yellow River, the sixth-longest river in the world. The river begins in northwest China and flows for 3,400 miles. It was here that the first Chinese people settled and began to create a culture.

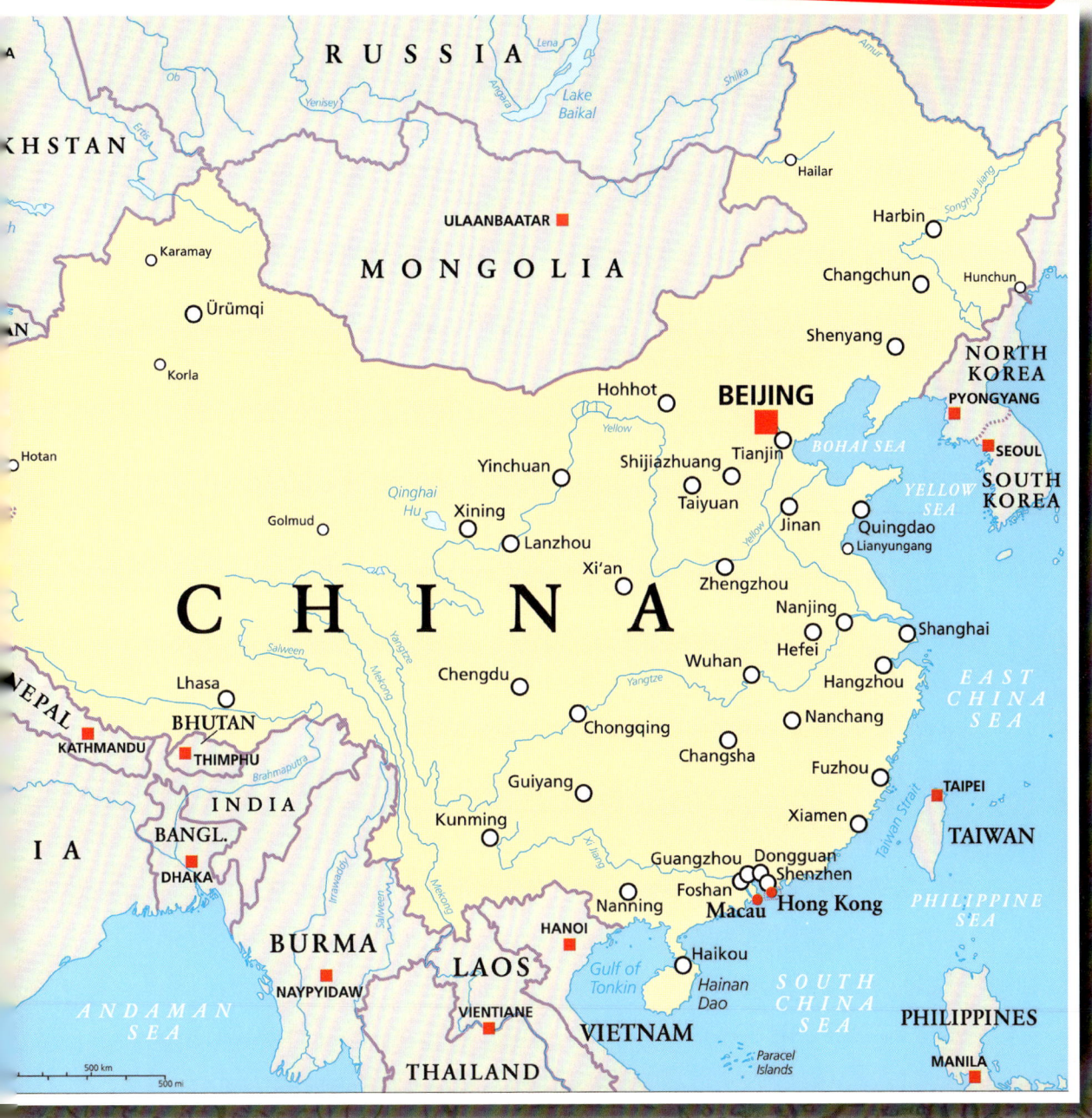

Throughout its long history, China's vast size has made it possible for many different groups of people to make their homes there.

A MYSTERIOUS CIVILIZATION

The Yellow River was the cradle, or birthplace, of ancient Chinese civilization. Little is known about these first Chinese people. The first culture was called the Longshan, but only scant archaeological evidence of how these people lived remains today. Archaeologists have discovered that the Longshans surrounded their villages with strong walls made of rammed (compacted) earth. Archeologists have found pieces of black pottery. They have also found graves where the bodies were buried with ceremonial items and wore jewelry.

The next civilization, the Xia dynasty, existed from 2205 BCE to 1570 BCE. Xia means "summer." The Xia did not leave any written records, so while archaeologists have discovered some things about their lifestyles, they don't know anything about their social and political lives. However, traditional Chinese history states that this was the time when all of the basic elements of civilization, such as agriculture, markets, and water control, were introduced to Chinese civilization.

Black pottery, such as this goblet, is just one of the items archaeologists have found from the Longshan culture.

STAYING AND FARMING

One of the features of the Yellow River Valley that made it the birthplace of Chinese civilization was the river itself. The river, which was fed by melting ice, did not flood as often as some of the other rivers in China. The Yellow River's waters were a reliable source of irrigation for farming, which was an important part of daily life. The soil, known as loess, was loose and made by deposited silt, or fine clay. This made it easy to work with simple primitive tools, which were made out of available materials such as animal antlers or stone.

All of these reasons made the area the ideal place for nomadic hunter-gatherer people to settle down and start using agriculture for growing the food that was necessary for their survival. The Longshan and Xia cultures started and grew out of these circumstances.

The Yellow River was the birthplace of China's ancient civilizations. Because this river did not flood as much as others, it made for a good place for people to settle.

HOME SWEET HOME

As the ancient Chinese people began to build villages, they also decided how to organize them, which suggests a lot about their daily lives. They grouped themselves into clans, or family groups. Large and small houses, a central meeting hall, storage pits, and wells for water were all surrounded by walls made of rammed earth. These hard-packed dirt walls were probably used for protection, which might also mean that neighboring villages may have been fighting each other. These villages may also have had special areas for worship or for upper-class citizens.

Houses were built on hard dirt floors, which may have been covered with mud plaster. They had wooden posts to support mats of woven reeds or bamboo for roofs. The walls were woven branches covered with mud plaster. Some houses were built of clay bricks, which were baked in ovens to make them hard. Clay bricks could also be built into stilts to protect houses from flooding.

Archaeologists digging in the Henan Province have found evidence of homes and palaces dating from the Xia period of ancient China.

WHAT'S FOR DINNER?

What did people eat every day in the Longshan and Xia cultures? When agriculture became common, they planted millet and rice. Millet grew well in the loess soil, while rice grew in wet paddy fields. Millet could be cooked as a kind of porridge. Rice was boiled in water as it still is today. Rice could also be made into wine. Later, people also grew wheat and a cereal plant known as sorghum. Soybeans were crushed and made into oil. They also ate tofu, or bean curd, as a kind of protein.

People ate fish as well as meat from sheep, cattle, and wild game animals. They also ate chicken and pork. Most poor people could not afford meat. Fruits included citron, apricots, and peaches. Bok choy and cucumbers both grew in China and supplied the people's daily diet with vegetables. These people also cooked their food in clay or bronze pots.

Millet, which could be grown in the loess soil, was one of the earliest grains planted by ancient Chinese farmers.

WHAT THEY WORE . . . AND MORE

During the Xia dynasty the arts of weaving cloth and making silk were first developed. This time was also when people first started to dress according to their social ranks. Peasants often wore clothing made from hemp, which was made from woven plant fibers. Hemp was durable for people who spent their days working in the fields. It was made into loose-fitting trousers and shirts that allowed for easy movement. The upper-class people wore robes made of silk, with long or short sleeves and sometimes with belts. The robes were usually long and sometimes dyed with designs.

Men wore their hair in a topknot, covered with a square of cloth or a hat. Women wore their long hair braided and coiled. Hair was seen as a sign of self-respect. It was as important as the body. Cutting or shaving hair was a terrible punishment because it insulted the soul.

Hemp plants provided the fiber to weave the cloth for everyday clothing, such as loose pants and shirts.

FROM XIA TO SHANG

The Shang dynasty came after the Xia dynasty, when the Shang leader overthrew the last Xia emperor. The Shang dynasty offers more archaeological evidence than the Xia. It was a time of technological advances, but also wars between city-states. It was an era that saw society divided into nobles and peasants in a feudal system. The nobles spent their days living in luxury while the peasants struggled to survive. Even the tombs of the nobility were ornate and filled with expensive items they might need in the afterlife.

The peasants were mostly farmers. They grew millet, wheat, rice, and barley and raised pigs, sheep, oxen, dogs, and silkworms. They did not own the land they worked. Instead, it was owned by a nobleman, who broke his land up into small plots. Peasant families farmed each plot, and these families were allowed to keep for themselves a small amount of the food they grew.

Sites such as this ancient town, which dates back to the Shang Dynasty, provide relics to help historians understand China's oldest cultures.

A DYNASTY OF INVENTIONS

The Shang dynasty is known for the many inventions that took place during that time. The people developed the ability to cast bronze into large, elaborate vessels like pots. They continued to develop a system of writing, which had just started during the Xia dynasty. This language had roughly one thousand characters, some of which are similar to the Chinese writing used today.

The Shang dynasty also used the new system of writing to create oracle bones. Scribes wrote questions on the shoulder blades of oxen or the flat undersides of turtle shells. Then the shells were heated until cracks formed. A diviner was thought to have special abilities that allowed her (or sometimes him) to see into the events of the future. She interpreted the cracks to find answers to the questions asked. Oracle bones are the best record of the Shang dynasty that historians have.

This ancient turtle shell is inscribed with the oracle bone characters that ancient Chinese used for telling the future.

INSIDE AND OUTSIDE THE CITY WALLS

People were still divided into clans, and their leaders were fighting over land and cities practically daily. Most of the population lived in or near walled cities, protected by walls of strong brick that could be 30 feet (9 meters) tall and 65 feet (20 m) wide. These walls might be miles long. Inside these walls, the nobility lived in palaces made from the same bricks or wood.

Craftsmen and merchants lived outside the walls in mud huts. They were not allowed to go inside the walls when there was an attack. Farmers lived in small villages that were scattered around the city. Their huts were made from mud, with packed earth floors and thatched roofs. These huts were usually just one room. In the summer, the peasants moved to temporary bamboo houses built on the plot of land that they farmed. In the winter they returned to their village homes.

This site, once a royal palace from the Shang Dynasty, has been excavated and preserved.

LIFE AT HOME

Family was an important part of Shang dynasty life. In both nobility and peasant families, the oldest male was the head of the household. Women were obedient to men, and children were required to show respect and never argue. If one member did something wrong, the reputation of the entire family was affected and all family members could be punished.

Clothing consisted mostly of robes. Men and women both wore knee-length tunics or shirts called *yi*, which were tied with a sash. A yi went over a narrow ankle-length skirt called a *chang*. The outfit also included a *bixi*, which was a length of cloth that reached the knees. The only colors weavers could make were red, blue, yellow, and green. In the winter, padded jackets were worn for warmth. Nobility might have more elaborate decorations on their clothing. Only the rich people wore silk. Poor people still wore loose shirts and pants made from hemp or ramie, another vegetable fiber.

湯

順天應人　本乎仁義
以賀維忠　匪曰求異
盤銘一徳　桑林六事
人紀肇修　垂千萬歲

This illustration shows King Cheng Tang, first king of the Shang Dynasty, wearing elaborate silk robes.

COOKING AND CHOPSTICKS

Shang dynasty people still ate millet, wheat, and rice. They used two types of millet: foxtail was eaten as a thick porridge, and panic was used in stews. They may also have made noodles from millet. They ate cattle, sheep, chickens, and pigs, as well as game animals like boar, water buffalo, and wild cattle. They may even have eaten raccoon, bamboo rats, rhinoceroses, elephants, and wolves. Shang people also ate clams, shrimp, and fish, as well as apricots and a fruit called medlar.

The Shang dynasty saw daily use of chopsticks. The earliest chopsticks were made of bronze and were probably used for cooking. Wooden chopsticks were developed, and people began using them to eat. Before the Shang era, chopsticks were not of equal length. The Shang standardized chopsticks as being two sticks of equal length. The Shang also used six different types of cooking pots, and they used special types of pots for food and beverage storage.

This bronze pot, found in a tomb in Henan, China, was used for cooking and also showed how wealthy the family was.

GODS AND ANCESTORS

Even though the social classes were separated by money and rank, religion was an important part of the daily lives of all Shang people. Shang Ti, which means "Lord on high," was the supreme god. He ruled over the smaller gods of things like the sun and the moon, as well as other natural forces. The Shang people sacrificed animals to Shang Ti and the other gods, for the health of their families and the success of their crops.

Worshipping ancestors was also important. The Shang people believed that dead ancestors in heaven were interested in the daily lives and affairs of their living families. If ancestors were not happy, the family would not be prosperous and terrible things could happen. Shang Ti was a link between people and their ancestors: the souls of these ancestors visited with Shang Ti and he told them what to do.

Shang Ti was worshipped on the Altar of Heaven in the imperial palace. All Shang people, including imperial rulers, worshipped him.

ENTER THE ZHOU

The Zhou dynasty evolved from the Shang and was one of the longest-lasting dynasties in all of Chinese history. It lasted about eight hundred years. This was a time of many technological advances that improved the daily lives of the Zhou people in all kinds of ways. Cast iron was invented, and it was used to create stronger and more durable weapons and tools, such as crossbows and iron plows. Farmers learned how to rotate crops to get the best production from their lands. They began growing soybeans as a major crop, too. Irrigation and water control also helped farmers keep their crops well watered.

The Zhou dynasty invented better communications and writing systems. The people also began building the first sections of the Great Wall of China. The Zhou dynasty began using metal coins for money, instead of shells or the barter system. Their coins were cast from bronze.

The Zhou Dynasty was the first to use metal coins made of bronze, such as these, for money.

POLITICS AND FAMILY

Under the Zhou dynasty, the emperor ruled over many smaller territories, which in turn were ruled by hereditary aristocrats. Peasants still worked the land under these lords, just as in the Shang period. Each peasant joined with all the other peasants to work plots of land for the nobleman. There may have also been slaves who worked for the nobleman as well. Some slaves may have been criminals or prisoners of war.

Family was even more important. This was partly because peasants were growing rice, which took a lot of labor. Families, including children, all had to work together to grow the rice they needed. Every family member had a specific place, and everyone worked for the good of the family. Every family member always obeyed the head of the family, who in turn conformed to the will of the king or emperor.

Emperor Wu-Ti ruled during the later part of the Zhou Dynasty. His rule extended over many smaller regions.

FARM AND FIELD

Under the feudal system, farming was managed in a very specific pattern. A piece of land would be separated into nine different squares, in the shape of the Chinese character known as *jing*, which means "water well": 井. The grain grown in the center square, which was tended by all the peasants, belonged to the nobleman. All of the squares around it were farmed by the individual farmers for their own daily food needs.

Because of new iron tools and water systems, Zhou farmers were growing crops that produced more food than before. Rice became more important, but it required a lot of hard work to grow. Seedlings had to be planted in water in a nursery bed, then transplanted to a rice paddy. It was harvested by carefully cutting the stalks and removing the kernels of rice. Farmers also grew corn, millet, broomcorn, and soybeans.

Rice grows well in watery rice paddies like this, but it requires hard work to cultivate.

LIVING AT HOME IN THE ZHOU DYNASTY

Social class still determined what kind of homes people lived in during the Zhou dynasty. Wealthy people lived in large homes or palaces constructed from wooden beams, with walls of rammed earth or brick. They had clay-tiled roofs, and the tiles were often decorated. These homes were built in a square, with a courtyard in the center. This brought natural light and ventilation into the building. The walls were thick, with usually just one entrance to the home. Furniture, for both nobles and peasants, was low to the ground. People squatted or sat on the floor on woven mats.

Peasants still lived in small huts of mud or bamboo, with earthen floor. Doors faced south to let in the sun's heat and light. A sunken pit in the middle of the floor was used for the fire that both heated the house and cooked food. Some homes were built partially underground for warmth during the winter.

King Mu of the Zhou dynasty is shown in his palace, being entertained by a woman playing a guzheng, a type of stringed musical instrument.

ZHOU DRESSED FOR CLASS

During the Zhou dynasty, peasant clothing did not change. People still wore simple garments made of hemp and ramie that could stand up to hard work in the fields. Men wore loose pants and cotton shirts. Women wore one-piece robes. Peasants went barefoot most of the time, but they had shoes of wood or straw for cold weather.

Nobles wore ornate robes, often of silk, and clothing was a symbol of social status. Only the emperor could wear the color yellow. The width of a robe's sleeves and the decoration on it also showed status and wealth. Some even wore extra decorations made of the green stone called jade, which would hang off their clothing. The wealthier Zhou people also wore jewelry. More ornaments meant the wearer had more wealth. Later, the *shenyi*, which was also called a "deep robe," became popular. It was a combination tunic and skirt.

A wealthy person of the Zhou Dynasty probably wore this jade pendant. Wealthier people wore more jewelry.

FOOD FOR PEASANTS AND KINGS

Many varieties of vegetables, fruits, and nuts were part of the Zhou diet. There were still many kinds of animals available for meat as well; in fact, there may have been around one hundred different animal options to include in this diet. This included the usual domesticated, or tame farm animals, such as sheep and cattle, as well as wild game and fish. There were also wines made from rice, sorghum, or millet. Members of the royal family and the government often ate large meals with all kinds of different courses and had hundreds of cooks to prepare them. Their food was usually of a higher quality than what the peasants ate.

Because of the advances in agriculture, most food now came from farmed crops and animals, instead of wild game and plants that could be foraged. However, peasants still ate more rice, cereal crops, and vegetables and rarely had meat.

This bronze spoon, called a *ch'ih*, was used to scoop wine from containers. Ancient Chinese made wine from rice, sorghum, or millet.

AN ANCIENT LEGACY

Many of the traditional Chinese ways of life got their start in the ancient civilizations of the Xia, Shang, and Zhou cultures. Drinking tea, eating rice and vegetables, using chopsticks, and wearing traditional Chinese robes all have their origins in these ancient cultures. Some of their practices, such as sacrificing animals or consulting oracle bones, are no longer performed in modern China, but these details in the history of their daily lives still remain interesting.

Even though the ancient Chinese cultures did not always leave written or archaeological records of their daily lives, their legacies live on in the foods, houses, clothing, and religious practices that continue today. Their inventions, including paper, gunpowder, and silk, have spread far beyond the borders of China to other parts of the world. That is quite an accomplishment for people who lived thousands of years ago.

This bronze sculpture of two wrestlers, from the Zhou Dynasty, is just one of the clues left about life in ancient China.

GLOSSARY

barter The system of trading goods and services without using money.
cast To make an object by shaping molten metal in a mold.
ceremonial Relating to or used for religious or public events.
characters Symbols used in a writing system, such as an alphabet.
city-state A city and its surrounding area that form an independent political state.
clan A group of families who are related or close-knit.
climate The weather conditions in an area over a long period of time.
dynasty A sequence of rulers from the same family or group.
feudal A legal and social system where peasants were protected and provided for by nobles in exchange for working for them.
fiber The thread or filament that makes up the tissue of a vegetable plant.
irrigation To supply land with water by artificial methods.
loess Loose yellow-gray sediment that is blown by the wind.
millet A kind of cereal plant that grows quickly and easily in warm areas with poor soil.
nomadic Roaming from place to place without a fixed home.
oracle An answer that reveals hidden knowledge or divine purposes.
plot An area of land that has been measured into distinct units or parts.
rotate To grow different crops in succession on a piece of land, to keep the soil from becoming exhausted.
silt Fine sand, clay, or other material that is carried by water and deposited in a channel or harbor.
sorghum A type of cereal plant that is part of the grass family.
terrain The physical features of a piece of land.
topknot A knot or twist of hair arranged on the top of the head.

FOR MORE INFORMATION

The Bowers Museum
2002 North Main Street
Santa Ana, CA 92706
(714) 567-3600
Website: http://www.bowers.org/index.php/exhibitions/current-exhibitions/157-ancient-arts-of-china-a-5000-year-legacy.html
The Bowers Museum promotes the arts of cultures all around the world. Its website includes information on the exhibit "Ancient Arts of China: A 5,000 Year Legacy."

The British Museum
Great Russell Street
London WC1B 3DG
United Kingdom
Website: www.ancientchina.co.uk
The British Museum features exhibits focused on the daily life in ancient China.

National Museum of China
16 East Chang'an Avenue
Dongcheng District
Beijing 100006, P. R.
China
Website: http://ancientchina.chnmuseum.cn/en/
Among many visual treats at the National Museum of China, the museum includes a permanent exhibit that features artifacts and exhibits on ancient China.

WEBSITES

Because of the changing nature of Internet links, Rosen Publishing has developed an online list of websites related to the subject of this book. This site is updated regularly. Please use this link to access the list:

http://www.rosenlinks.com/SRFAC/cdaily

FOR FURTHER READING

Collins, Terry. *Ancient China: An Interactive History Adventure*. Minneapolis, MN: Capstone Press, 2012.

Deady, Kathleen W. *Ancient China: Beyond the Great Wall*. Minneapolis, MN: Capstone Press, 2011.

Demuth, Patricia Brennan. *Where Is the Great Wall?* New York: Grosset & Dunlap, 2015.

Friedman, Mel. *Ancient China*. New York, NY: Scholastic Books, 2010.

Hile, Lori. *Daily Life in Shang Dynasty China*. Portsmouth, NH: Heinemann, 2015.

Holm, Kirsten. *Everyday Life in Ancient China*. New York, NY: Rosen Publishing, 2012.

Liu-Perkins, Christine. *At Home in Her Tomb: Lady Dai and the Ancient Chinese Treasures of Mawangdui*. Watertown, MA: Charlesbridge, 2014.

Ransom, Candace. *Tools and Treasures of Ancient China*. Minneapolis, MN: Lerner Publishing, 2014.

Sonneborn, Liz. *Ancient China*. New York, NY: Children's Press, 2012.

Steele, Philip. *Hands-On History! Ancient China*. Helotes, TX: Armadillo, 2013.

BIBLIOGRAPHY

Ancient China Life. "Ancient Chinese Peasants." 2009 (http://www.ancientchinalife.com/ancient-chinese-peasants.html).

Cambridge University Library. "Chinese Oracle Bones" (http://www.lib.cam.ac.uk/mulu/oracle.html).

China FashioNation. "Detailed Histories of Chinese Dynasties and Their Fashions" (http://chinafashion.weebly.com/detailed-histories-of-dynasties.html).

China Internet Information Center. "The History of Chinese Imperial Food" (http://www.china.org.cn/english/imperial/25995.htm).

Chinasage. "The Early History of China before 770 BCE." October 13, 2015 (http://www.chinasage.info/dynastyearly.htm).

Cultural China. "Ancient Chinese Clothing." 2014 (http://traditions.cultural-china.com/en/215Traditions9827.html).

Donn, Lin. "Shang & Chou Dynasties." MrDonn.org (http://china.mrdonn.org/shang&chou.html).

Ducksters.com. "Ancient China: Clothing." January 2016 (http://www.ducksters.com/history/china/clothing.php).

Duiker, William J., and Jackson J. Spielvogel. *World History*. Cengage Learning, 2015 (https://books.google.com/books?isbn=1305537785).

Eating Utensils. "Chopsticks History" (http://www.eatingutensils.net/history-of-other-eating-utensils/chopsticks-history/).

Hooker, Richard. "Ancient China: The Shang." World Cultures, 1997 (http://richard-hooker.com/sites/worldcultures/ANCCHINA/SHANG.HTM).

Hujiang.com. "A History of Chinese Hair Style." September 23, 2013 (http://cn.hujiang.com/new/p533598/).

The Human Journey. "Ancient Settlements: China" (http://www.humanjourney.us/china2.html).

Independence Hall Association. "Shang Dynasty: China's First Recorded History," 2014 (http://www.ushistory.org/civ/9b.asp).

Karr, Karen. "Food in Ancient China." Quatr.us, 2016 (http://quatr.us/china/food/).

Lo, Yu-Ngok. "Siheyuan and Hutongs: The Mass Destruction and Preservation of Beijing's Courtyard Houses." American Institute of Architects. November 19, 2010 (http://www.aia.org/practicing/AIAB086563).

Newman, Jacqueline M. "Shang Dynasty Foods." *Food in History,* Spring 2006 volume, 13(1), pp. 7 and 16 (http://www.flavorandfortune.com/dataaccess/article.php?ID=548).

Schinz, Alfred. *The Magic Square: Cities in Ancient China*. Edition Axel Menges, 1996 (https://books.google.com/books?isbn=3930698021).

Silberman, Neil Asher. *The Oxford Companion to Archaeology*. New York, NY: Oxford University Press, 2012 (https://books.google.com/books?isbn=0199735786).

Wertz, Richard R. "Exploring Chinese History: Ancient Era." Ibiblio.org, 2016. Retrieved December 18, 2015 (http://www.ibiblio.org/chinesehistory/contents/01his/c01s01.html).

INDEX

A
agriculture, 4, 6, 8, 12, 38
ancestor worship, 26

B
bronze, 12, 18, 24, 25, 28–29, 41

C
cast iron, 28
chopsticks, 24, 40
clans, 10, 20,
coins, 28–29,
crossbows, 28

G
Great Wall of China 28
gunpowder, 40

L
Longshan
  food 8, 12
  people 6, 8

P
paper, 40
plows, 28

R
rice 12, 16, 24, 30, 32–33, 39–40

S
Shang dynasty, 16
  clothing, 22–23
  family life, 22
  food, 16, 24
  religion, 26–27
slaves, 30

W
writing, 18, 28

X
Xia dynasty 6, 8, 16, 18
  clothing, 14
  food 12,
  people, 6

Z
Zhou dynasty, 28, 40
  clothing, 36
  family, 30
  food, 32, 38
  housing, 34
  inventions, 28, 40
  religion, 40

ABOUT THE AUTHOR

Marcia Amidon Lusted has written 125 books and more than 500 magazine articles for young readers. She often writes about ancient history and has traveled to several ancient sites around the world.

PHOTO CREDITS

Cover, p. 1 Linghe Zhao/Photodisc/Getty Images; p. 3 Hou/Moment/Getty Images; p. 5 © iStockphoto.com/PeterHermesFurian; pp. 7, 37 DEA Picture Library/De Agostini/Getty Images; p. 9 Wolfgang Kaehler/LightRocket/Getty Images; pp. 11, 17, 21 Sovfoto/Universal Images Group/Getty Images; p. 13 JTB Photo/Universal Images Group/Getty Images; p. 15 Sean Gallup/Getty Images; p. 19 Heritage Images/Hulton Archive/Getty Images; p. 23 Pictures from History/Bridgeman Images; p. 25 © China Images/Alamy Stock Photo; p. 27 Private Collection/Archives Charmet/Bridgeman Images; p. 29 STR/AFP/Getty Images; p. 31 ullstein bild/Getty Images; p. 33 Visions of America/Universal Images Group/Getty Images; p. 35 Culture Club/Hulton Archive/Getty Images; p. 39 DEA/L. De Masi/De Agostini/Getty Images; p. 41 Print Collector/Hulton Archive/Getty Images; cover, p. 1 dragon graphic father/Shutterstock.com; back cover and interior pages background map Marzolino/Shutterstock.com; cover and interior pages background textures and patterns zffoto/Shutterstock.com, Elena Larina/Shutterstock.com, llaszlo/Shutterstock.com

Designer: Michael Moy; Editor: Heather Moore Niver; Photo Researcher: Heather Moore Niver